The Amazing Human Body

The Respiratory System

KRYSTYNA PORAY GODDU

BLACK RABBIT BOOKS

Bolt is published by Black Rabbit Books
P.O. Box 227, Mankato, Minnesota, 56002.
www.blackrabbitbooks.com

Jennifer Besel, editor; Grant Gould, designer;
Omay Ayres, photo researcher

Library of Congress Cataloging-in-Publication Data
Names: Goddu, Krystyna Poray, author.
Title: The respiratory system / by Krystyna Poray Goddu.
Description: Mankato, Minnesota : Black Rabbit Books, [2019]
Series: Bolt. The amazing human body | Audience: Age 9-12.
Audience: Grade 4 to 6. Includes bibliographical references and index.
Identifiers: LCCN 2017021261 (print) | LCCN 2017022316 (ebook)
ISBN 9781680725070 (ebook) | ISBN 9781680723915 (library binding) |
ISBN 9781680726855 (paperback)
Subjects: LCSH: Respiration–Juvenile literature.
Classification: LCC QP121 (ebook) | LCC QP121 .G54 2019 (print)
DDC 612.2-dc23
LC record available at https://lccn.loc.gov/2017021261

Image Credits

Alamy: Brain light, 3, 25; DonSmith, 4–5; MARIE SCHMITT / BSIP, 11; Scott Camazine, 28; Dreamstime: Skypixel, 22; Science Source: Sophie Jacopin, 14–15; Shutterstock: Alexilusmedical, 1, 6–7; Alila Medical Media, 18 (b); Aspen Photo, 21; BlueRingMedia, 16–17, 31; Life science of anatomy, 12; Maridav, 32; mavo, 26–27; Meilun, 19; Nerthuz, 8; Ralf Juergen Kraft, Cover (skeleton); Sebastian Kaulitzki, Cover (skeleton), 29; stefanolunardi, 23; Tefi, 18 (t); Vector for u, Cover (bkgd)
Every effort has been made to contact copyright holders for material reproduced in this book. Any omissions will be rectified in subsequent printings if notice is given to the publisher.

CONTENTS

CHAPTER 1

BREATHING in and Out

A boy takes a breath. Then he lets it out. It doesn't matter if he's awake or sleeping. Breathing happens over and over again.

People have to breathe to stay alive. Many body parts work together to breathe. Those parts are the respiratory system.

PARTS OF THE RESPIRATORY SYSTEM

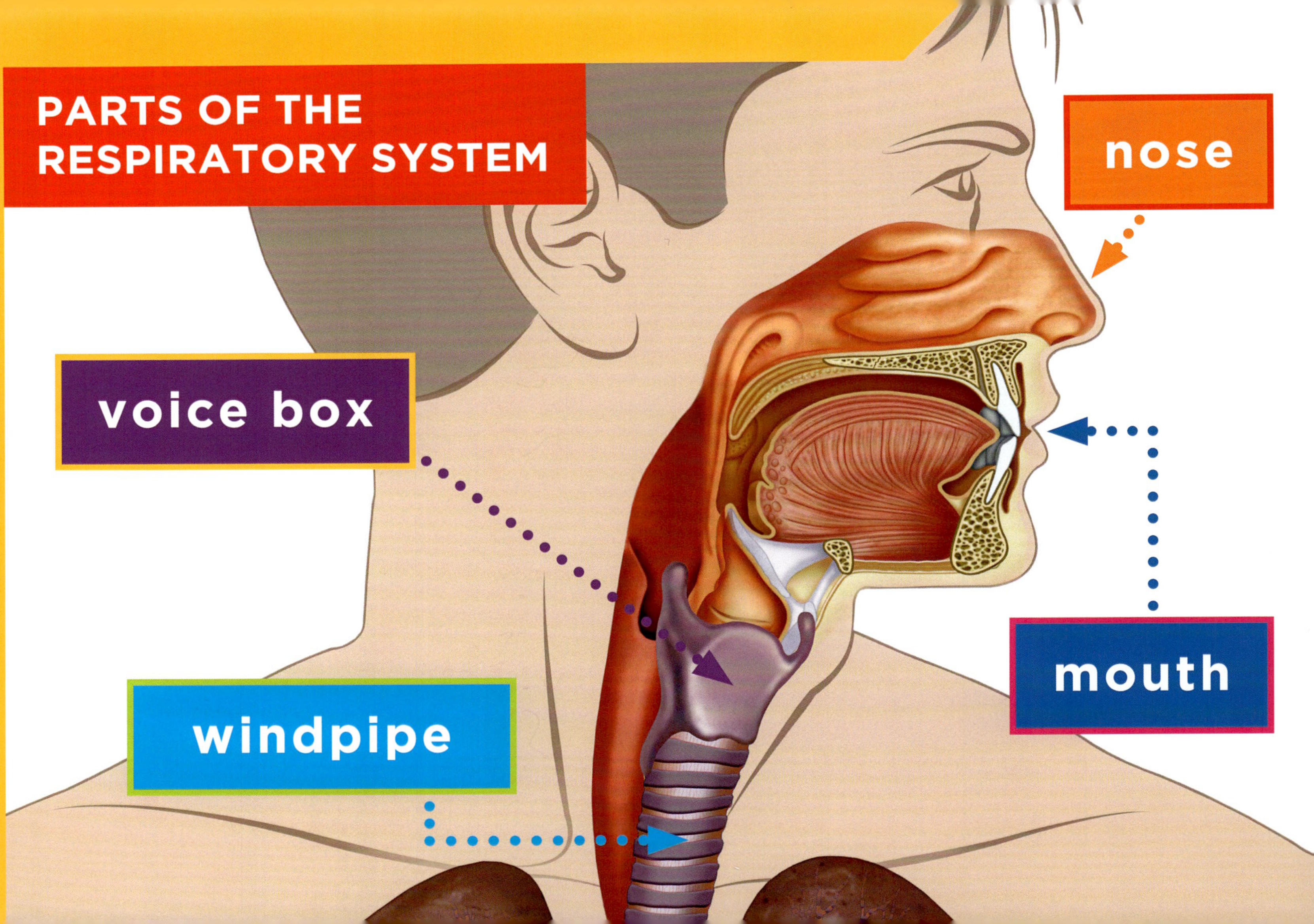

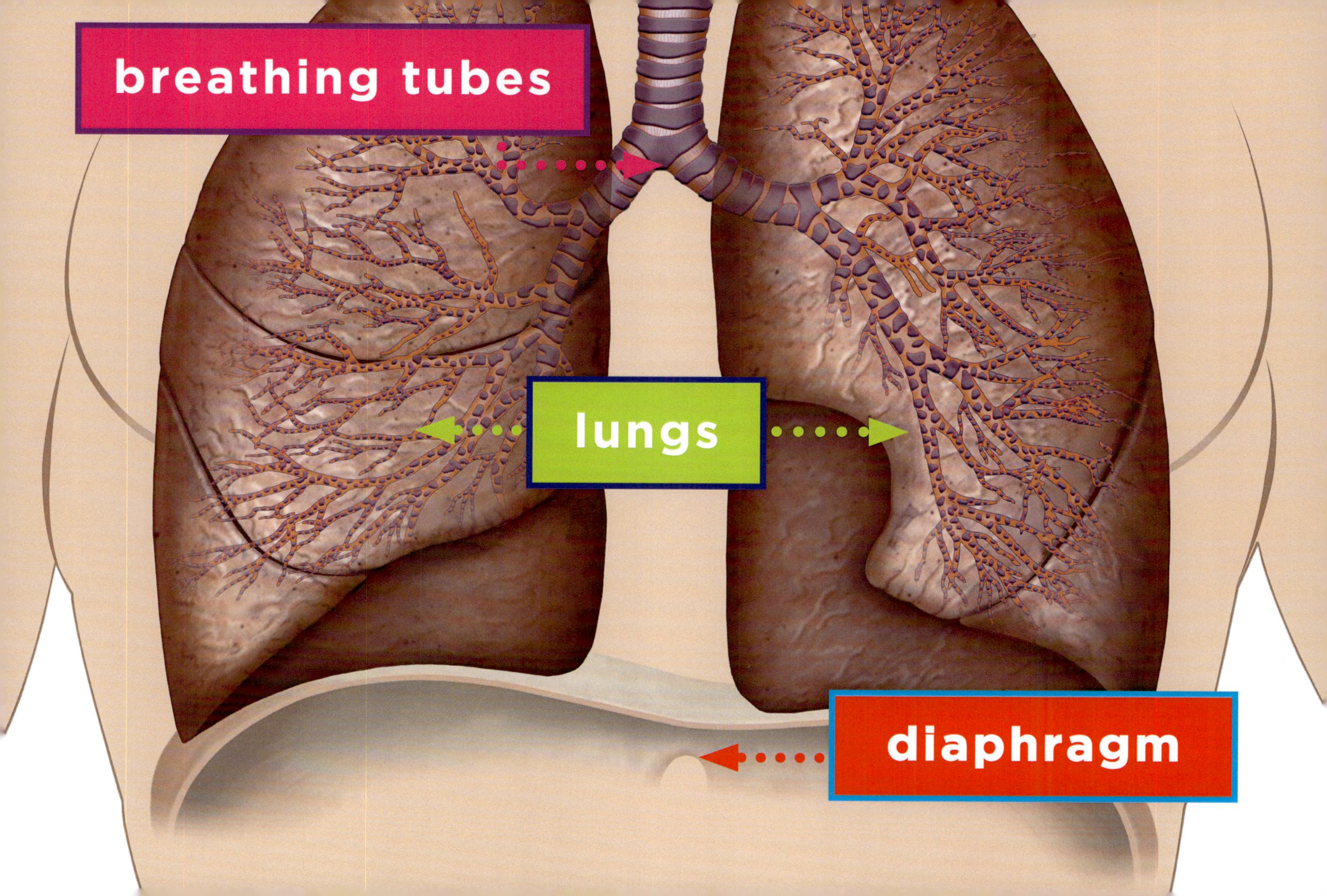
breathing tubes
lungs
diaphragm

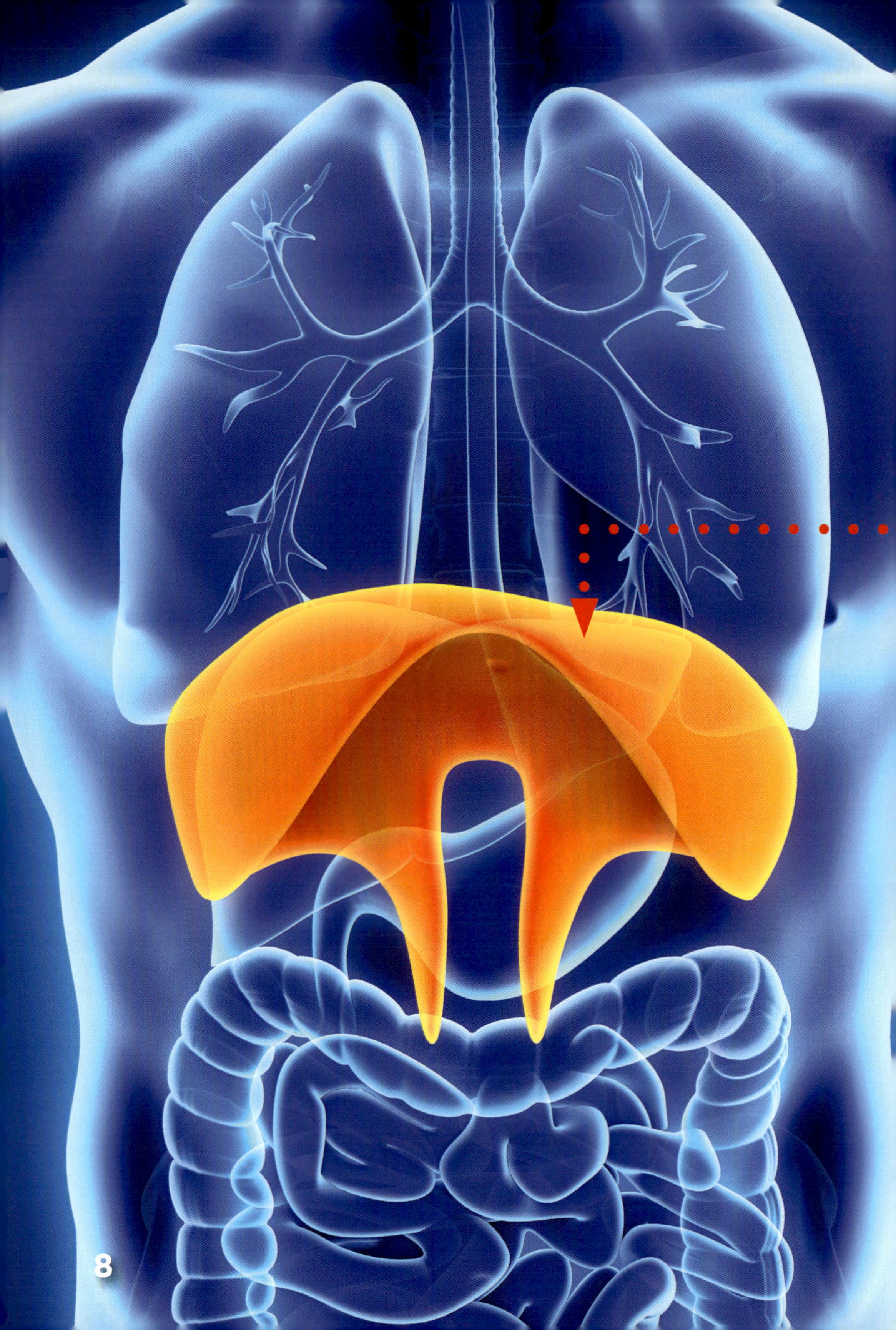

The Brain and Muscles

People don't have to think about breathing. The respiratory system works on its own. The process starts with the brain. The brain sends signals to the diaphragm and other muscles. It tells those muscles to tighten. That tightening makes a person breathe in. To **exhale**, the brain tells the muscles to relax.

CHAPTER 2

The Trip to the LUNGS

People breathe for an important reason. Air contains **oxygen**. The body's **cells** need oxygen to work.

Air comes in through the nose and mouth. It travels down the throat to the voice box. From the voice box, it continues through the windpipe.

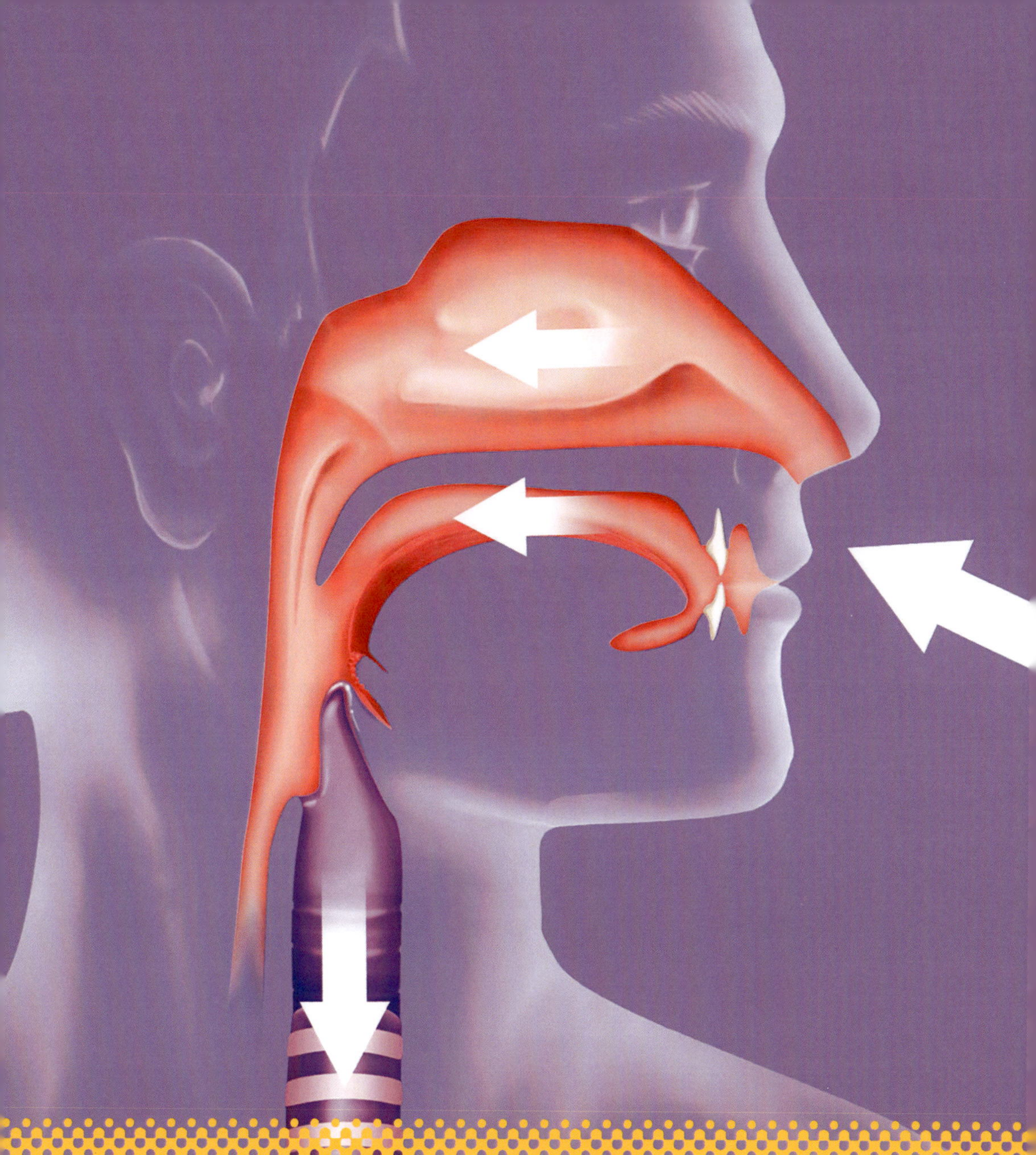

Tiny hairs line the inside of the nose. These hairs stop dirt and dust from getting into the body.

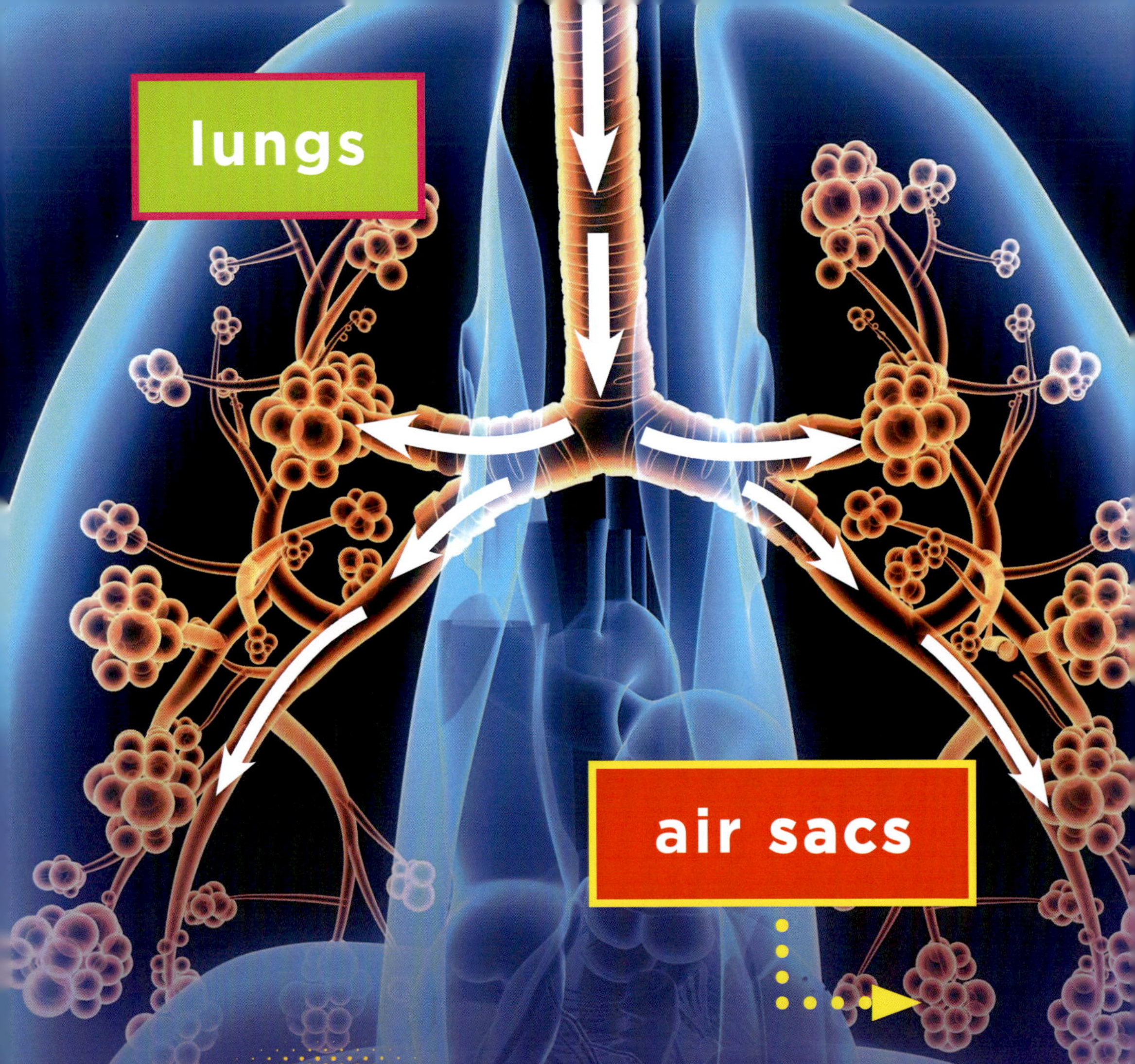
lungs
air sacs

COMPARING BREATHING RATES
dog
adult human
tortoise
approximate breaths per minute
0
5

The Breathing Tubes

Air travels from the windpipe into two breathing tubes. Those tubes connect to the lungs. In the lungs, the tubes branch into smaller tubes. The smallest tubes end in millions of tiny sacs. Air fills those sacs.

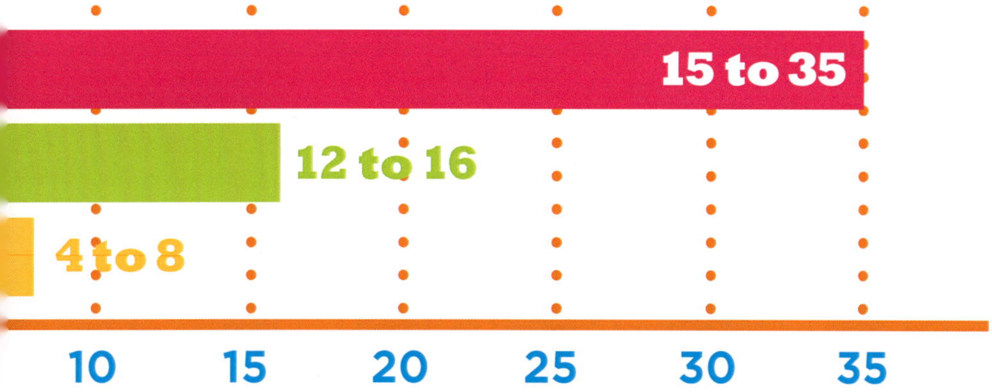

In the Lungs

Once in the body, oxygen has to get into the blood. That job happens in the lungs. Blood **vessels** surround the air sacs. The sac walls are very thin. Oxygen goes through the walls. It then passes into the blood vessels.

Blood vessels carry oxygen-filled blood to the heart. The heart then pumps it throughout the body.

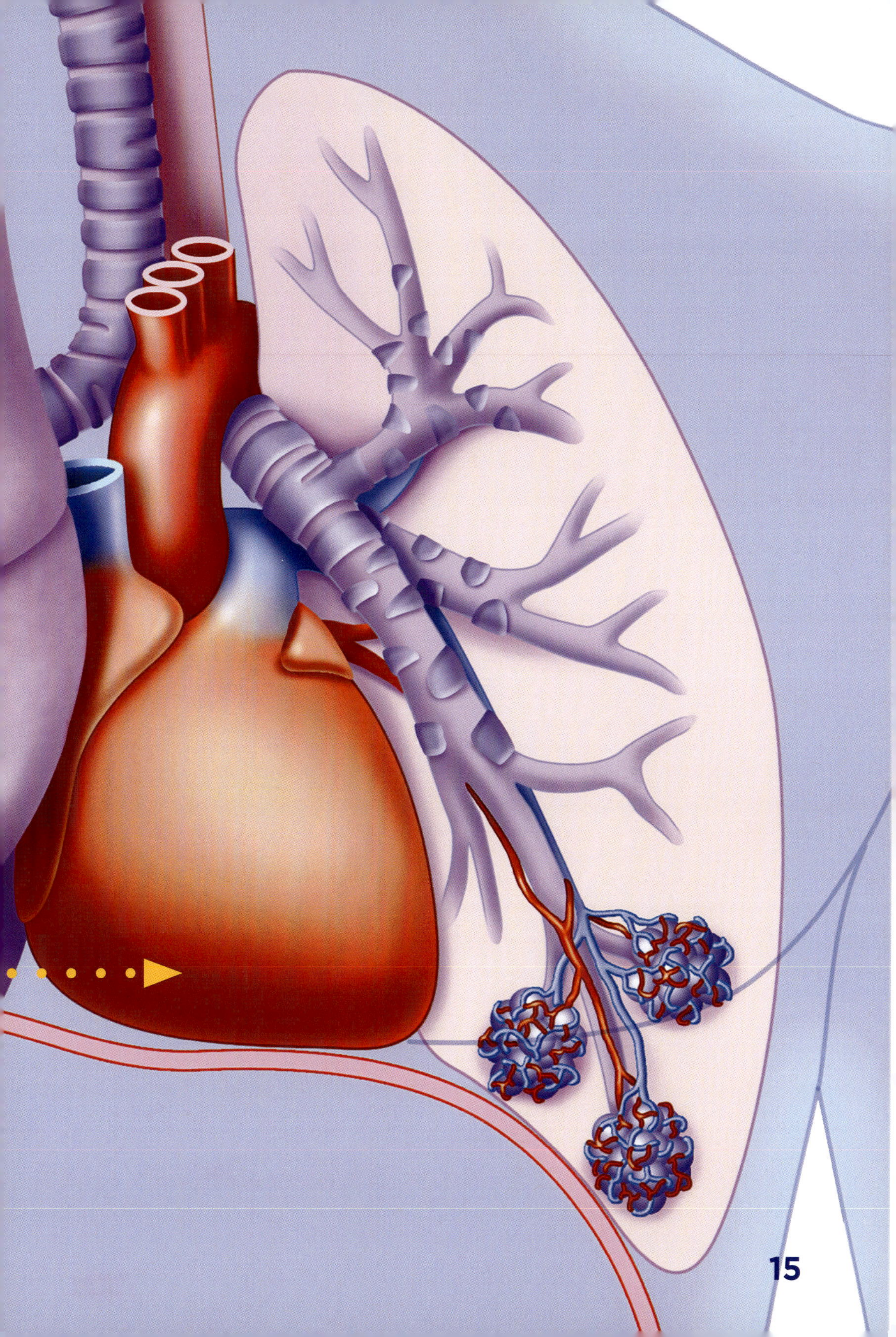

TRAVELING THROUGH THE LUNGS

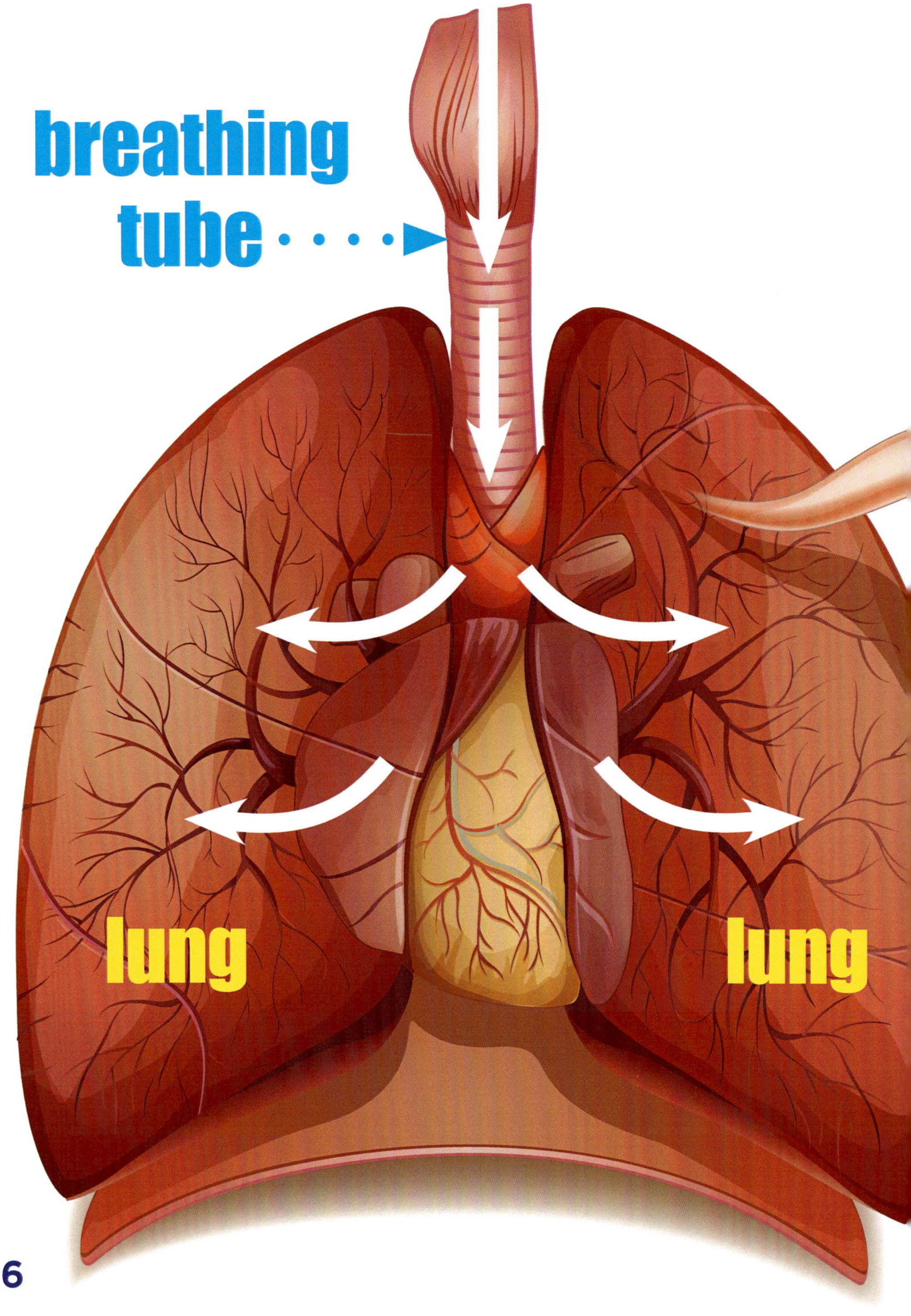

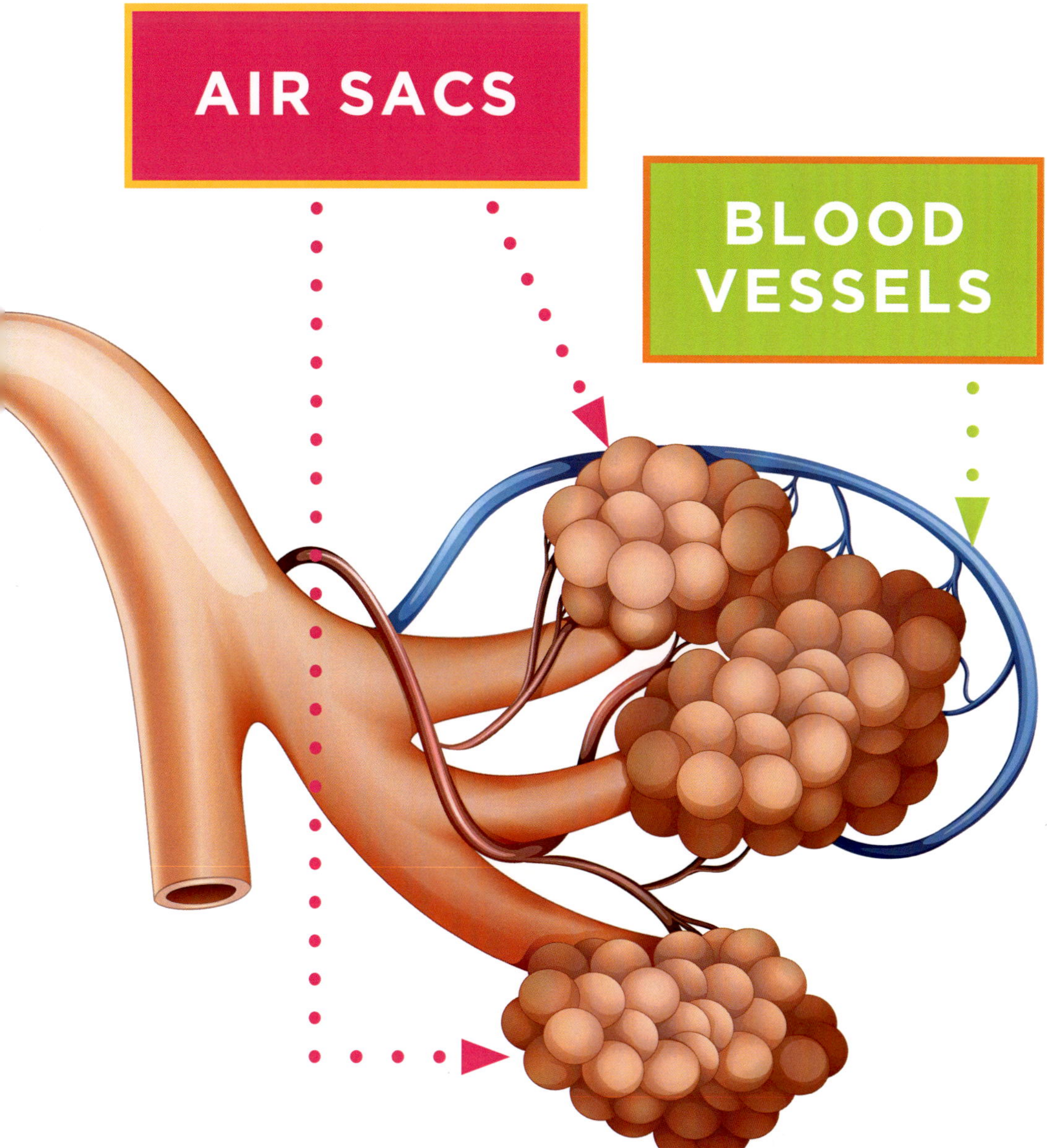
AIR SACS
BLOOD VESSELS

The Path Out

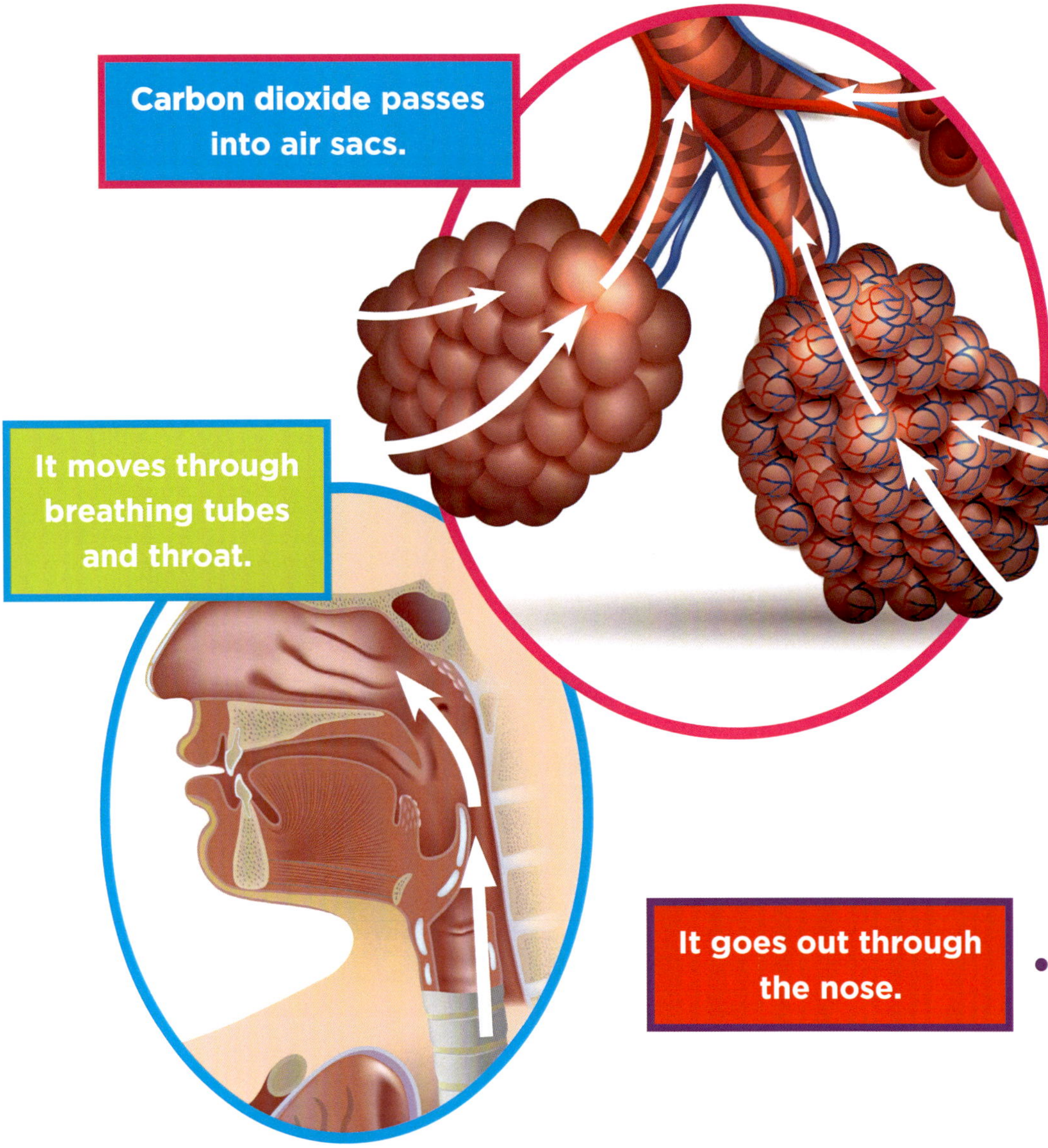
Carbon dioxide passes into air sacs.
It moves through breathing tubes and throat.
It goes out through the nose.

CHAPTER 3

BREATHING Out

Cells use oxygen for energy. But as they use it, cells create carbon dioxide. This gas needs to get out of the body. Carbon dioxide passes into the air sacs. In an exhale, the gas comes out.

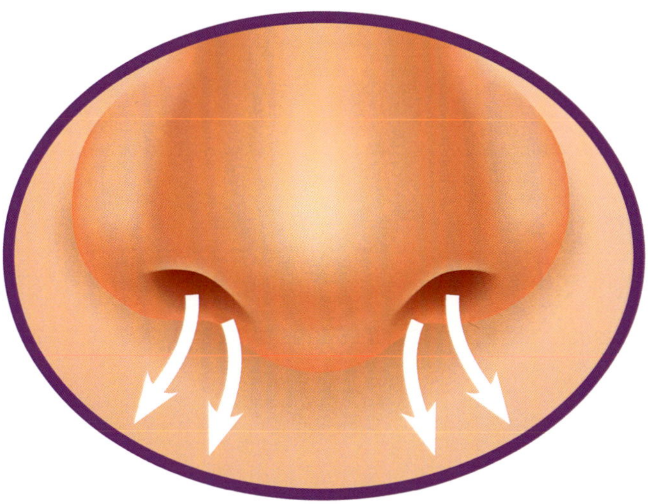

Breathing Faster

Exercise causes cells to use more oxygen. They also make more carbon dioxide. When there's too much carbon dioxide, the body reacts. The brain tells the respiratory system to work faster. The person breathes more quickly.

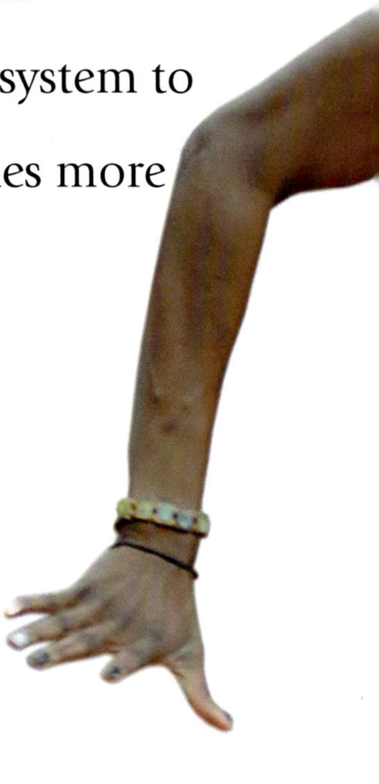

A person breathes up to 23,040 times a day.

PENN RELAYS
AM
VT
PENN RELAYS
AM

CHAPTER 4

Built-In PROTECTIONS

Dirt, dust, and germs sometimes sneak into the body. But the body fights back! Sneezing is one protection. When dust tickles nose hairs, the brain responds. It tells muscles to squeeze and push the dust out. Achoo!

Cough It Out

Coughing gets rid of things that don't belong too. Chest and abdomen muscles force air and germs out. The air from a cough travels very fast.

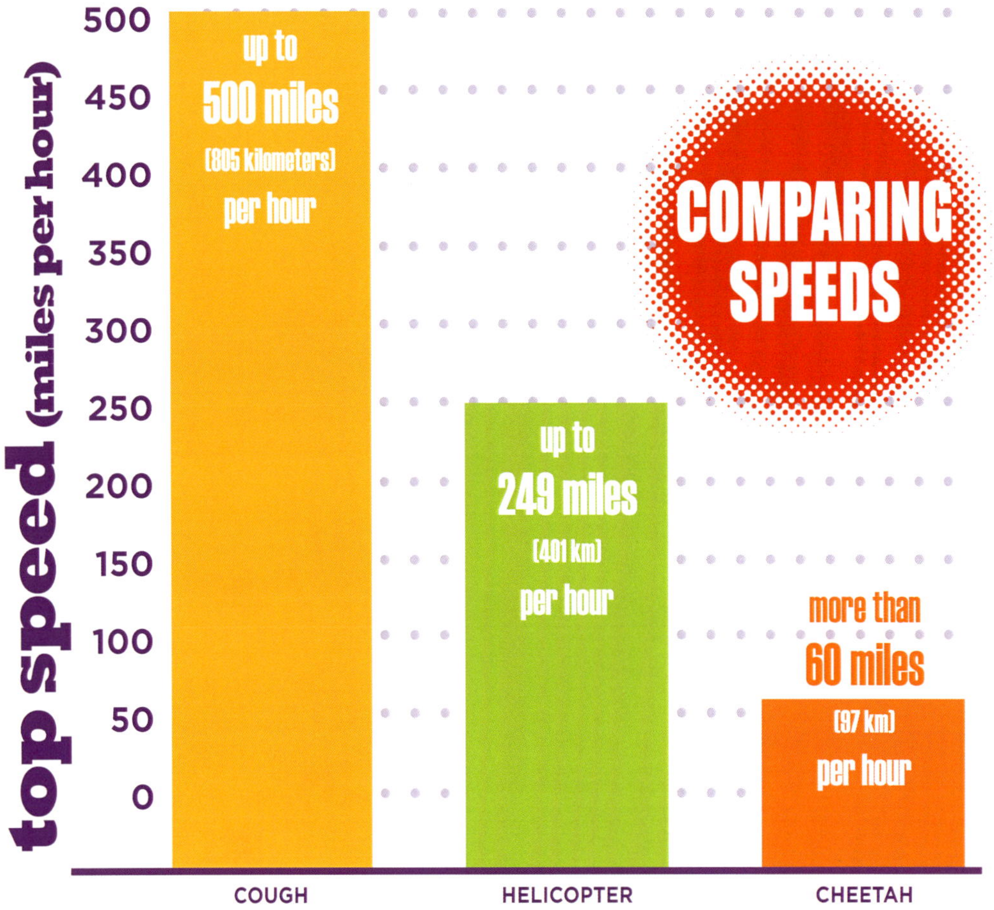

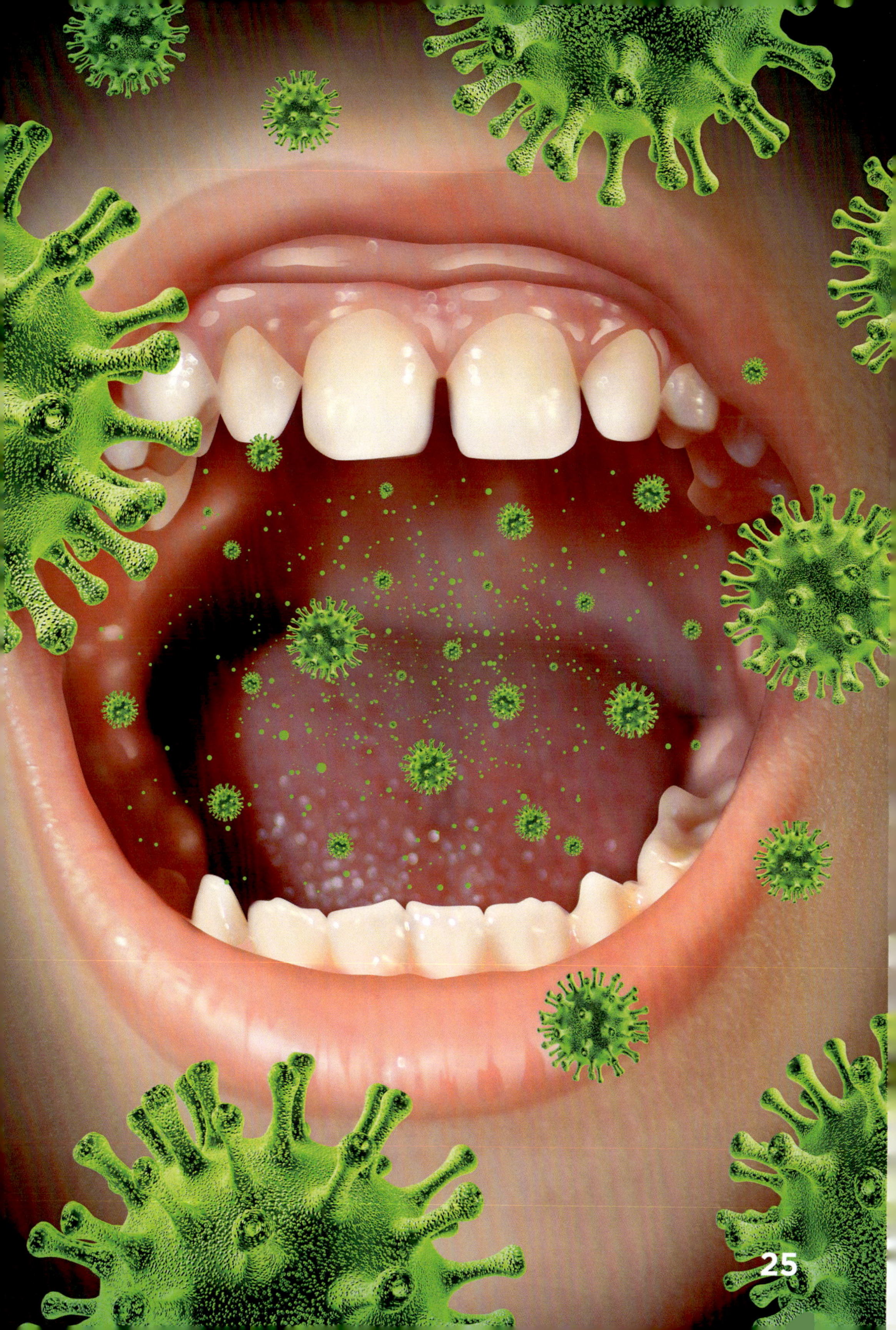

CHAPTER 5

A System in ACTION

People can survive without food for days. But they can only live a few minutes without breathing. Take a deep breath. That's the respiratory system in action.

BY THE NUMBERS

up to
26 feet
(8 meters)
distance droplets go from a sneeze

about
3,000 GALLONS
(11,356 liters)
AMOUNT OF AIR A PERSON BREATHES EACH DAY

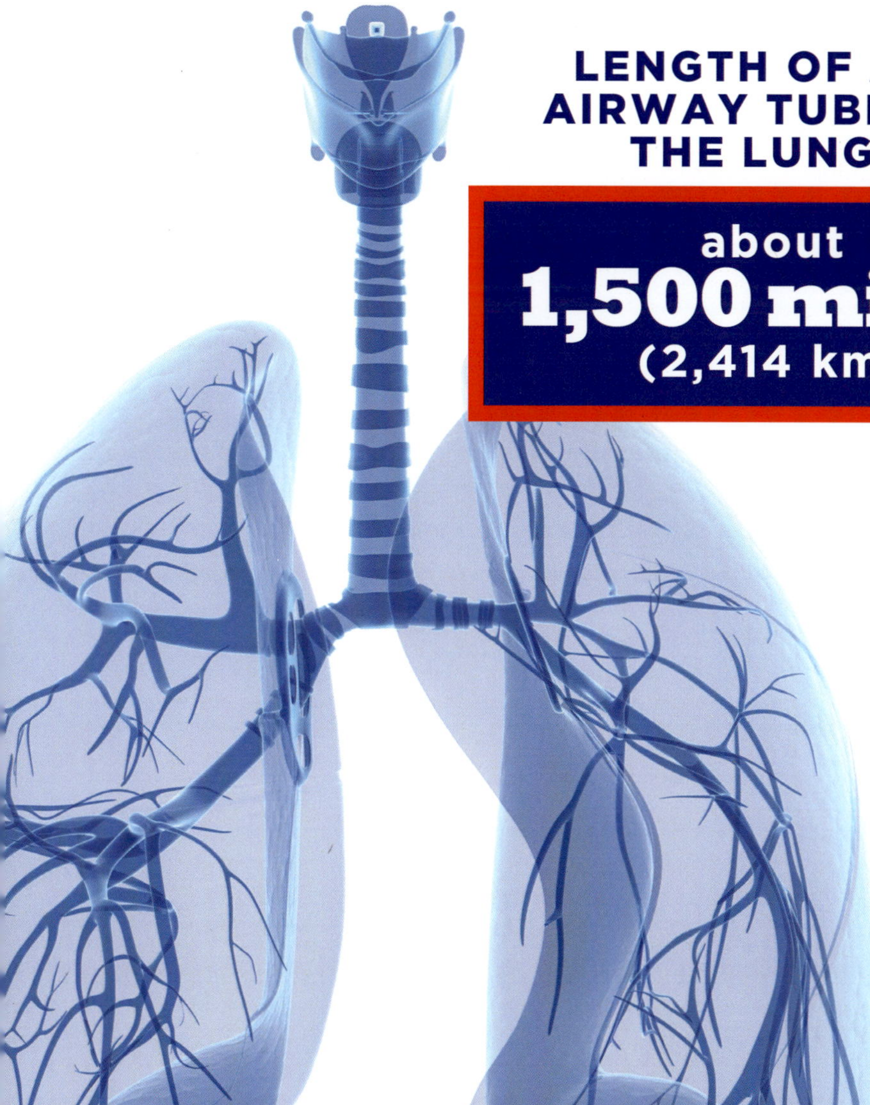

LENGTH OF ALL AIRWAY TUBES IN THE LUNGS

about
1,500 miles
(2,414 km)

at least
441,504,000
number of breaths a 70-year-old person has taken

GLOSSARY

carbon dioxide (KAR-buhn dy-AHK-siyd)—a colorless gas that is formed in the process of breathing

cell (SEL)—one of the tiny units that are the basic building blocks of living things

diaphragm (DY-uh-fram)—the main muscle used for breathing in humans

exhale (eks-HAYL)—to breathe out

oxygen (AHK-si-jin)—a gas that is necessary for life

sac (SAK)—a part inside the body of an animal or plant that is shaped like a bag and usually contains liquid or air

vessel (VEH-suhl)—a tube in which a body fluid is contained and flows through

LEARN MORE

BOOKS

Kenney, Karen Latchana. *Respiratory System.* Amazing Body Systems. Minneapolis: Jump!, Inc., 2016.

Mason, Paul. *Your Breathtaking Lungs and Rocking Respiratory System: Find Out How Your Body Works!* Your Brilliant Body! New York: Crabtree Publishing Company, 2016.

Rose, Simon. *Respiratory System.* How the Human Body Works. New York: AV2 by Weigl, 2015.

WEBSITES

Breathing and the Respiratory System
www.ducksters.com/science/breathing.php

Breathing System Facts for Kids
easyscienceforkids.com/all-about-human-breathing-system/

Your Respiratory System
discoverykids.com/articles/your-respiratory-system/

INDEX